D0917372

Holiday Punches
Party Bowls and soft drinks

Compiled by Edna Beilenson

Pictures by ♥ Vee Guthrie

Peter Pauper Press
Mount Vernon, N.Y.

COPYRIGHT 1953
PETER PAUPER PRESS

Greetings!

Some mortals need spirits
For holiday cheer,
But we can be gala
Without wine and beer;

We bring our high spirits
To make the drinks gay,
With nary a hang-over
The following day!

Decorative Punches for Festive Occasions

Decorative Punches

Party Tea Punch

   1 pint pitted sweet cherries
   2 quarts freshly boiling water
   3 tablespoons tea
   ½ cup chopped fresh mint leaves
   1 quart lemon ice
   Sugar
   Orange slices
   Lemon slices

Pour boiling water over tea; cover. Let stand 5 minutes; strain. Sweeten slightly. Add cherries and mint. Cover; chill several hours. Pour over ice in Punch bowl; add lemon ice. Garnish with orange and lemon. 25 servings.

Lemon or Orange Ice Punch

Put lemon or orange ice in the Punch bowl and add ginger ale in the proportion of 1 quart of ginger ale to each pint of the ice. Raspberry, pineapple, or any other water ice or sherbet can be substituted.

White Angel Punch

½ pint sugar sirup
1 pint lemon juice
1 quart strong tea
2 quarts white grape juice
2 quarts club soda

Prepare like any other Punch, adding the soda at time of serving. 50 servings.

Blue Angel Punch

Same as White Angel, but use black tea and ordinary purple grape juice.

Golden Dawn Punch

1 pint apricot sirup
1 pint lime juice
3 pints orange juice
3 quarts club soda

Prepare and serve same as the Angel Punches. One quart of juice from canned apricots can be used in place of one pint of sirup. 45 servings.

Ginger Punch

> 1 quart cider
> ½ cup shredded pineapple
> 1 orange, sliced thin
> 3 sprigs of mint, crushed
> 1 quart ginger ale
> 1 pint carbonated water

Mix cider and fruit. Add mint. Before serving add the remaining ingredients. 20 servings.

Many a slip twixt cup and lip!

Reception Punch

8 cups sugar
2 quarts water
½ cup crushed mint leaves
2 quarts iced tea
2 gallons water
2 quarts ginger ale
Mint sprigs and orange and lemon slices
3 quarts orange juice
1 quart pineapple or grape juice
1 quart lemon juice

For 5 minutes, boil sugar with 2 quarts of water. Add crushed mint leaves. Cool and strain. Add tea, fruit juices and remaining water. Just before serving time, add ginger ale. Pour over ice into Punch bowls. 160 servings.

Grape-Tea Cup

1 cup strong cold tea
4 slices canned pineapple
1 tablespoon lemon juice
1 pint grape juice
1 cup pineapple juice

Blend tea, pineapple and lemon juice in electric blender. Pour all ingredients into a pitcher partially filled with ice and stir. 8 servings.

Cardinal Punch

    4 cups fresh cranberries
    4 cups water
    2 cups sugar
    1 cup strained orange juice
    1 ½ tablespoons lemon juice
    1 quart ginger ale

Boil fresh cranberries in water until they are very soft. Crush and strain through cheesecloth. (Or use 4 cups bottled, or fresh frozen concentrated cranberry juice cocktail.) While hot, stir in sugar. Add strained orange juice and lemon juice. Chill until ready to serve, then add ginger ale and ice. 20 servings.

Cider Punch

    1 cup sugar
    ½ teaspoon grated nutmeg
    3 cups water
    2 cups cider
    4 cups ginger ale
    1 cup grapefruit juice
    3 slices lemon
    2 cups grape juice

Boil water, sugar and nutmeg together for 5 minutes. Cool. Add other ingredients. Pour over ice cubes. 24 servings.

Pineapple Lime Punch

    2 cups currant jelly
    2 cups boiling water
    2 cups pineapple juice
    ½ cup lemon juice
    ½ cup orange juice
    2 cups strained lime juice
    1 quart ginger ale

Beat currant jelly with rotary beater until frothy; add hot water and beat until jelly is dissolved; add fruit juices and chill. Before serving, add ginger ale and pour over ice. 25 servings.

Apricot Punch

    ½ pound dried apricots
    ½ cup sugar
    1 cup orange juice
    3 tablespoons lemon juice
    1 cup sweet cider
    1½ to 2 quarts iced water

Soak apricots 1 hour in water to cover, then stew until soft. Add sugar, cook 5 minutes longer, and sieve. Combine fruit juices and cider, pour over apricots and stir thoroughly; strain and dilute with iced water to taste. Garnish with candied cherries. 20 servings.

11

Cranberry Punch

   1½ cups sugar
   3 cups boiling water
   2 cups cranberry sauce
   ⅓ cup lemon juice
   1 pint raspberry ice
   1 quart carbonated water
   ½ cup maraschino cherries

Dissolve sugar in hot water, add sauce and stir until smooth; add lemon juice and strain through fine sieve or cheese-cloth; chill. When ready to serve, pour over block of ice in Punch bowl; add raspberry ice, carbonated water and cherries, chopped fine. 24 servings.

Tea Punch

Combine 4 cups strong, freshly brewed tea (made by using 2 teaspoons tea to 1 cup of boiling water) with 4 cups white grape juice and 8 tablespoons of lemon juice. Garnish with orange slices, straw-berries, pineapple sticks or other fresh fruit. Pour over a lump of ice in a large Punch bowl. This makes a 2-quart Punch, about 16 servings.

Christmas Wassail

2 quarts of sweet cider
Juice of 4 lemons and 4 oranges
1 cup granulated sugar
½ teaspoon ground nutmeg
1 ½ teaspoons allspice
1 teaspoon cloves
4 sticks cinnamon

Heat spices and cider together. Add other juices. Place 4 baked and quartered apples in bottom of wassail bowl. Pour over cider and juice mixture. Serve hot. 16 servings.

Old-fashioned Wassail

4 apples
¾ cup sugar
¼ cup water
6 cups apple cider
1 teaspoon allspice

Core apples, sprinkle with ¼ cup sugar, add water and bake in moderately hot oven (375°) 30 minutes or until tender, basting several times with sirup in the pan. Combine cider, remaining sugar and allspice and place over low heat, stirring until sugar is dissolved. Do not boil. Pour over roasted apples in the Punch bowl. Approximate yield: 6 portions.

Easy Fruit Punch

Mix 2 quarts of strong tea with 1½ quarts of grape juice, 2 cups lemon juice, 4 cups orange juice, 2 quarts water and 1 cup of sugar. Chill. When ready to serve add 1 quart of ginger ale and pour over ice in a Punch bowl. Float slices of lemon and orange, whole strawberries and maraschino cherries in the bowl, if desired. 64 servings.

Prohibition Punch

    1 cup water
    2 cups sugar
    1 cup orange pekoe tea
    6 oranges
    5 lemons
    2 cups crushed pineapple and sirup
    4 cups ginger ale

Boil sugar and water together for 10
minutes before adding the cup of tea,
juice of lemons and oranges and crushed
pineapple and sirup. Strain. Add 1 cup
of ice and the ginger ale and chill thoroughly. More water may be added if
you wish. Also, to "party-up" the
Punch, a cup of halved maraschino
cherries or whole strawberries may be
floated in the bowl. 12 servings.

Hollywood Parade

    1 quart orange juice
    1 quart orange sherbet
    1 quart vanilla ice cream
    1 quart ginger ale

Beat first three ingredients with beater
until well mixed. Add chilled ginger
ale. Stir and serve at once. 25 servings.

Fruit Punch with Lemon Ice

  1½ quarts water
  1½ cups sugar
  1 cup lemon juice
  1 quart strong tea
  2 cups orange juice
  Grated rind of 1 lemon
  3 quarts ginger ale
  1 quart lemon ice

Mix juices, sugar, tea and water and chill 12 hours or overnight. Add ginger ale just before serving over lemon ice. Float slices of lemon in the drink for decorative purposes. 60 servings.

Lime-Tea Punch

Steep 4 teaspoons tea in 1 cup boiling water for 5 minutes. Strain. Add 1 cup of light corn sirup and mix well. Add 4 cups of ice water and 1 cup of chilled lime juice. Just before serving, add 1 quart of ginger ale and pour over ice in a Punch bowl. Garnish with lime slices. 20 servings.

Hot Drinks

Hot Spiced Cranberry Juice

¾ cup brown sugar, firmly packed
1 cup water
¼ teaspoon salt
¼ teaspoon nutmeg
½ teaspoon cinnamon
½ teaspoon allspice
¾ teaspoon cloves
2 cans jellied cranberry sauce
3 cups water
1 quart pineapple juice
Cinnamon sticks
Butter or margarine

Bring to a boil sugar, water, salt, spices. Crush cranberry sauce with fork. Add water and beat with rotary beater until smooth. Add cranberry liquid and pine-apple juice to hot spiced sirup and heat to boiling. Serve hot. Dot with butter or margarine. Serve with cinnamon stick stirrers. Yields 2 ½ quarts.

Hot Fruit Punch

1½ cups sugar, dissolved in
2 cups strong tea (pour 2 cups
  boiling water over 8 teaspoons tea)
1 cup lemon juice, heated
5 cups orange juice, heated
2 quarts boiling water
Orange and lemon slices

Combine, and serve hot. 35 servings.

Hot Mulled Cider Punch

6 quarts cider
2 teaspoons whole cloves
A few sticks cinnamon
½ teaspoon nutmeg
¾ cup sugar

Combine the cider, cloves, cinnamon, nutmeg and sugar; bring to boil for 5 minutes; strain. Serve hot. 48 servings.

Hot Lemonade

6 lemons
1 cup sugar sirup, made from
  ½ cup sugar and ½ cup water
3½ cups boiling water

Squeeze juice from lemons, combine with sugar sirup and add boiling water. Serves 6.

Mulled Cider

¾ cup firmly packed brown sugar
¼ teaspoon salt
1 teaspoon cloves
1 teaspoon allspice
3 sticks cinnamon
Grated nutmeg
2 quarts sweet cider

Thoroughly mix brown sugar, salt and spices; add to sweet cider and simmer 10 minutes; strain through cheesecloth and reheat. This is best served steaming hot in earthen mugs. Serves 8.

Hot Tea

Use 1 or 2 teaspoons tea leaves for each cup of freshly boiling water; use tea bags or tea leaves directly from tightly covered canister. Fill tea pot with boiling water; drain when heated thoroughly. Place tea in pot, add freshly boiling water, cover and steep in warm place 3 minutes. Stir. Pour through strainer into preheated serving pot or into cups.

Variations: Serve with lemon slices stuck with cloves, raspberry conserve, ginger or oranges.

Steeped Party Coffee

Put 1 pound ground coffee, medium grind, in cheesecloth or muslin bag, allowing space for coffee to double in bulk. Drop bag into large kettle containing 2 gallons freshly boiling water; cover tightly and let stand over low flame 10 minutes. Remove bag, cover tightly and keep hot; it should be made just before serving. Coffee made thus is delicately flavored and particularly suitable for large gatherings. Serves 40.

Creole Coffee

¼ cup coffee, drip grind
2 cups boiling water
1 tablespoon cocoa or chocolate

Place a drip coffeepot in a pan of very hot water. Place coffee, mixed with cocoa, in middle section of pot (French-type drip coffeepot), which is kept scalding hot. Pour boiling water, 1 tablespoon at a time at 3- to 4-minute intervals, over the coffee, covering pot between intervals. When dripped through, serve with sugar to taste. Yield: 2 cups. A French-type drip coffeepot must be used.

Turkish Coffee

4 tablespoons coffee, pulverized
4 tablespoons sugar
2 cups water

Place coffee, sugar and water in a coffeepot. Heat and stir until mixture comes to a brisk boil and is very frothy. Remove from heat and let the froth subside; replace pan on a higher heat. Repeat this three times. Before serving, settle the grounds by adding a little cold water. Yield: 2 cups of coffee.

Café Espresso

⅓ cup coffee, drip-grind
5 cups boiling water
1 egg white
2 tablespoons sugar
¼ pint heavy cream

Prepare strong drip coffee by the usual method. Beat egg white until foamy. Beat in sugar. Whip cream lightly but not until stiff. Fold the two together and top each cup of coffee with fluffy white caps. Place the lump of sugar in cup before pouring coffee. Sugar may be omitted. Serves 6.

Café au Lait

French Café au Lait: Make *double* strength coffee by any method desired. Have ready an equal quantity of freshly scalded milk. Simultaneously pour the coffee and milk in equal amounts into heated cups.

If a richer drink is desired, top each cup with 1 tablespoon whipped cream. *Café au Lait* is the French breakfast coffee traditionally served with *croissants* or *brioches.*

Hot Cocoa

 ⅓ cup sugar
 6 tablespoons cocoa
 Dash of salt
 1 cup water
 5 cups milk

Combine sugar, cocoa and salt in saucepan; stir in water and boil 2 minutes, stirring until thickened. Add milk and heat slowly until scalded and just below the boiling point; cover and keep hot over hot water; before serving, beat with rotary beater until frothy. Serves 6.

Spiced Cocoa

 ½ cup cocoa
 ½ cup sugar
 Dash of salt
 1¼ teaspoons cinnamon
 4 cups water
 2 cans evaporated milk
 1 teaspoon vanilla extract
 Whipped cream

Mix together cocoa, sugar, salt and cinnamon; add water. Bring to boiling point; boil 3 minutes. Add milk; heat. Beat with rotary beater until frothy; add vanilla extract. Top with cream.

Hot Chocolate

2 squares bitter chocolate
1 cup cold water
Dash of salt
3 tablespoons sugar
3 cups milk

Heat together chocolate and water, stirring until chocolate is melted and blended; add salt and sugar and boil 4 minutes, stirring constantly. Place pan

Polar bears
And Eskimos
Sip cold drinks......
To warm their toes

over hot water, gradually stir in milk, and heat thoroughly. Beat with rotary beater until frothy. Serves 6.

Mexican Chocolate

4 squares bitter chocolate
1 cup boiling water
2 cups condensed milk
4 cups water
6 tablespoons sugar
Pinch of salt
Pinch of allspice
½ teaspoon nutmeg
2 teaspoons cinnamon
2 eggs
2 teaspoons vanilla

Cut up or coarsely grate bitter chocolate into 1 cup boiling water, and stir over the fire until it is blended. Add condensed milk and 4 cups water, sugar, the merest pinch of salt, allspice, nutmeg, and cinnamon. Cook this in the top of a double boiler for 1 hour, beating with a rotary beater at least a half-dozen times during the cooking. Beat eggs and add them the last time the chocolate is whipped. Add vanilla just before removing from heat. Serves 8.

Broadway Chocolate

2 squares bitter chocolate
½ cup coffee infusion
1 cup sugar
3 cups milk
1 teaspoon vanilla
Whipped cream

Heat chocolate and coffee together, stirring until chocolate is melted and blended. Cook 2 minutes, stirring constantly. Add sugar and milk and cook slowly 5 minutes. Flavor with vanilla and serve with a spoonful of whipped cream in each cup. Approximate yield: 6 portions.

Party Chocolate

⅓ cup heavy cream, whipped
4 cups milk, scalded
¾ cup chocolate sirup

Fold cream into cold chocolate sirup; place 1 heaping tablespoon in each serving cup and fill with hot milk, stirring until well blended; serve at once. Approximate yield: 6 portions.

For Chocolate Sirup, refer to recipe on page 39.

French Chocolate

  3 squares bitter chocolate
  ½ cup sugar
  1 cup water
  4 cups milk, scalded

Grate chocolate, add sugar and water and cook gently over boiling water 20 minutes; stir in hot milk and serve at once. Approximate yield: 6 portions.

Christmas Wassail

See recipes pages 13 and 14.

Frosty Drinks for Hot Weather

Frosty Drinks

Raspberry Mint Crush

2 cups sugar
3 cups boiling water
1 cup red raspberries
1 bunch mint
2 cups lime juice

Dissolve sugar in hot water and chill; add berries, crushed with mint and lime juice, and chill 2 to 3 hours in refrigerator. Strain and pour over cracked ice in small glasses and serve with additional mint leaves. Makes 12 small glasses.

Planters Punch

2 cups orange juice
2 cups lemon juice
2 cups Grenadine
3 quarts ginger ale
Rum flavoring, to taste
Strawberries, sliced pineapple

Mix juices, flavoring, sugar, water and chill 12 hours or overnight. Add ginger ale just before serving over ice. Garnish with mint leaves. 60 servings.

Lime Rickey

Juice of 1 large lime
1 teaspoon sugar
Charged water

Stir lime juice and sugar together in an 8-ounce glass, add 2 large ice cubes, fill glass with charged water and stir again. Garnish with slices of lime.

Grape Juice Lime Rickey

Juice of 1 small lime
2 ounces grape juice
1 teaspoon sugar

Stir together in an 8-ounce glass, add 2 large ice cubes, fill the glass with charged water, stir again, and serve with stirring rod.

Kumquat Rickey

Juice of 3 kumquats
1 teaspoon sugar
Charged water

Stir kumquat juice with sugar in an 8-ounce glass. Add 2 large ice cubes, and the shell of half a squeezed kumquat. Fill glass with charged water and stir again. Serve garnished with mint leaves.

Grape Juice Fix

8 parts grape juice
2 parts lemon juice
1 part pineapple sirup

Mix ingredients and serve in tall glass over cracked ice. Garnish with mint leaves.

On certain occasions
A tall drink is best;
For longer enjoyment
It tops all the rest

Pineapple Daisy

- 1 part Grenadine
- 2 parts lime or lemon juice
- 8 parts pineapple juice

Mix ingredients and pour into goblet over cracked ice. Serve decorated with pineapple sticks and fresh strawberries, if available.

Raspberry Daisy

- 1 part Grenadine
- 2 parts lemon juice
- 8 parts raspberry sirup

Mix ingredients and pour into prepared goblet over cracked ice. Float whole fresh raspberries in this drink for an effective party-like look.

Dummy Daisy

- 1 part Grenadine
- 2 parts lemon or lime juice
- 8 parts orange juice

Mix and pour into prepared goblet and stir with cracked ice. Decorate with orange slices and a sprig of mint for gala occasions.

Mint Cooler

Crush 1 or 2 sprigs of mint with 1 or 2 teaspoonfuls sugar in the bottom of the glass, add the ice, decorate with lemon peel, and fill glass with ginger ale.

Lone Tree Cooler

Juice of 1 lemon and ½ orange with 1 ounce Grenadine. Fill up with charged water.

Spicy Coffee Cooler

    15 whole cloves
    2 sticks cinnamon
    ½ cup ground coffee
    7 cups boiling or cold water
    1 cup powdered sugar
    1 tablespoon granulated sugar
    1 cup heavy cream, whipped
    Cinnamon

Add cloves, cinnamon and coffee to water and brew as usual; strain and add powdered sugar. Pour into tall glasses half filled with crushed ice; top with sweetened cream and dust with cinnamon. Serves 6.

Iced Coffee

Prepare coffee twice the usual strength.
Pour hot coffee over cracked ice in tall
glasses, or over block of ice in large
pitcher. Serve with plain or whipped
cream and sugar or serve black.

Austrian Iced Coffee

Half fill tall glasses with cracked ice,
sprinkle powdered sugar over ice, as desired, and place 1 tablespoon whipped
cream in each glass. Pour hot strong
coffee into iced glasses.

Iced Café au Lait

Pour 1 cup double strength coffee over
cracked ice in tall glass; add small scoop
vanilla or coffee ice cream; serve at once.

Iced Café-Chocolat

Shake or beat thoroughly 1 cup strong
coffee, 1 tablespoon chocolate sirup, 2
tablespoons whipped cream and 3 tablespoons chipped ice. Serve at once.

Frosted Coffee

Half fill 6 tall glasses with chopped ice; pour hot strong coffee over ice until glasses are three-fourths full, and top each with a heaping tablespoon of vanilla ice cream. Use 1 quart hot coffee for 6 glasses.

Coffee Delight

4 cups iced coffee
1 cup whipping cream
8 tablespoons sugar sirup
1 quart ginger ale

Mix coffee and sirup. Fill 8 tall glasses ¼ full of crushed ice. Whip cream; into each glass put ¼ cup cream, ½ cup coffee mixture and ½ cup ginger ale. Stir.

Iced Tea

Prepare strong tea, using 1 ½ teaspoons per cup. Pour hot tea over cracked ice in tall glasses. Or pour hot tea over block of ice in large pitcher. Tea is clearer and more sparkling cooled quickly than cooled slowly. Garnish with lemon or orange slice.

36

Iced Ginger Tea

Boil ginger root in water 2 to 5 minutes, or until water is flavored as desired; strain, use boiling hot liquid for preparing strong tea. Proceed as for Iced Tea.

*Christmas in a Torrid clime
Feels cooler with a Glass of lime*

Spiced Iced Tea

 2 cups sugar
 2 cups water
 5 teaspoons black tea
 5 mint leaves
 1 teaspoon allspice
 1½ cups strained orange juice
 ¾ cup strained lemon juice
 4 quarts iced water

Boil sugar and water 5 minutes; add tea, mint and spice; cover lightly and let stand 15 minutes; strain and add fruit juices. Pour over cracked ice, add the water and serve. Serves 15 or 20.

Mint Julep Iced Tea

To 2 cups tea infusion, add 1 bunch mint, crushed, 6 tablespoons lemon juice, ¾ cup sugar and 3 whole cloves; chill several hours. When ready to serve, strain and add 1 pint white grape juice, ¼ cup each diced pineapple and sliced maraschino cherries, 1 orange sliced thin, then cut in eighths, and 1 quart carbonated water. Pour into tall glasses half filled with cracked ice and top with sprig of fresh mint. Makes 15 tall glasses.

Chocolate Sirup

1 ½ cups hot water   ⅛ teaspoon salt
1 ½ cups sugar   1 teaspoon vanilla
6 squares bitter chocolate

Melt chocolate over hot water, stir in hot water, sugar and salt and cook about 5 minutes, stirring until smooth; cool and add vanilla. Pour into glass jar, cover tightly and store in refrigerator. For chocolate drinks, use 2 tablespoons for 1 cup milk. Yields 2 cups sirup.

Iced Chocolate

Use 2 tablespoons chocolate sirup to 1 cup milk; beat with rotary beater or shake until frothy and pour over cracked ice in tall glasses. Flavor with cinnamon, ginger, a drop of peppermint extract, or crushed mint leaves, and serve with whipped cream. Yields 1 large glass.

Iced Russian Chocolate

Mix ½ cup cold black coffee, ¼ cup chocolate sirup and 1 cup boiling water. Pour over cracked ice and serve in a tall glass garnished with whipped cream.

Oriental Chocolate

4 cups ginger ale
½ pint vanilla ice cream
½ cup cocoa

Pour the ginger ale into shaker. Then add cocoa and ice cream and shake vigorously. Pour into tall glasses. Serves 6.

Iced Chocolate Mocha

2 cups strong coffee
6 cups milk
1 cup chocolate sirup
½ cup heavy cream, whipped

Combine hot coffee, milk and chocolate sirup; beat with rotary beater until frothy; cool. Pour over chopped ice in small glasses and top with whipped cream. Serves 12.

Iced Mint Cocoa

Mix ½ cup cocoa and 1 cup sugar with 4 cups boiling water. Add 3 sprigs crushed mint, and chill. Add 1 teaspoon vanilla and pour into tall glasses, half filled with crushed ice. Top with whipped cream and garnish with mint. Serves 6.

Special Drinks for Children's Parties

Children's Drinks

Sneaky Peek

This is a teen-age favorite, and can turn out to be delicious or poisonous according to the ingredients used. As may be guessed from the name of the drink, the ingredients must be mixed under the table, in a sneaky fashion, and none of the guests may peek. They have to drink the finished product on faith. Usually ginger ale is one of the ingredients used, and to it may be added sarsaparilla, grape juice, cream soda, orangeade or raspberry sirup.

Any or all of the above may be used, and in any sickening proportion desired!

Sneaky Peek is a big hit at teen-age parties and usually the drink does not turn out as badly as might be expected, if the bartender can be persuaded to use a little discretion. The name derives from a Bowery drink of more intoxicating ingredients, called Sneaky Pete.

Ice-Cream Soda

 2 ounces sirup (of flavor desired)
 1 ounce milk
 2 scoops ice cream
 Carbonated water
 Whipped cream, if desired

Combine sirup and milk in tall glass, add ice cream, and fill glass with carbonated water. Mix well. Top with whipped cream.

Vanilla Ice-Cream Soda: Use simple sugar sirup (half sugar and half water) with a dash of vanilla flavoring.

Chocolate Ice-Cream Soda: Use chocolate sirup. (See page 39).

Fruit or Berry Ice-Cream Sodas: Use fruit or berry sirup, increasing quantity to 3 ounces for fuller flavor.

Lemonade

 1 tablespoon sugar sirup
 Juice of 1 large lemon

Combine and pour into tall glass full of cracked ice. Fill glass with either plain or charged water, stir thoroughly, decorate with fruits, and serve.

Egg Lemonade

Plain lemonade with the addition of 1 whole egg. Shake the lemon, sugar, and egg thoroughly in a shaker; pour into glass without straining; add the water, stir, and serve.

Orangeade

Use 1 large or 1½ to 2 small oranges in place of lemon. A combination of either lemon or lime with the orange greatly improves the drink.

Limeade

Use 2 large limes in place of lemon.

Lime-Lemonade, Lime- or Lemon-Orangeade

Prepare like plain lemonade but with mixed fruit juices as follows:

- (a) ½ large lemon, 1 large lime
- (b) 1 large orange, 1 lime
- (c) 1 large orange, ½ lemon

All sorts of juices have all sorts of uses...

Pink Circus Lemonade

6 cups lemon juice (3 dozen lemons)
6 cups sugar sirup
2 ¾ gallons water
Red coloring

Mix the lemon juice with the sugar sirup. Then add the water and stir thoroughly. Add the red coloring until the lemonade turns pink. Makes approximately 50 servings.

Milk Shake, Milk Punch

1 whole egg
½ pint sweet milk
Sugar to taste (1 to 3 teaspoons sirup)

Shake with cracked ice until thoroughly blended and chilled, then strain into tall glass. Dust with ground nutmeg.

Banana Milk Shake

1 ripe banana
1 cup cold milk

Slice banana into a bowl and beat with an egg beater or electric mixer until smooth and creamy. Add milk and mix thoroughly. Serve cold. Makes 2 glasses.

Banana Frosted
Milk Shake

Add 3 tablespoons vanilla ice cream before mixing.

Banana Chocolate
Milk Shake

Add 1 tablespoon chocolate sirup before mixing.

Banana Spiced
Milk Shake

Sprinkle nutmeg on top of banana milk shake just before serving.

Orange Milk Shake

2½ cups orange juice
1½ cups grapefruit juice
1 cup evaporated milk
1 cup water
½ teaspoon salt
¼ teaspoon almond extract
¼ cup sugar
1 cup cracked ice

Combine all ingredients in shaker; shake until well mixed. Yields 6 tall glasses.

Chocolate Milk Shake

Add 1 tablespoon chocolate sirup to basic milk shake recipe on page 46, before shaking.

Frosted Chocolate

Use 2 tablespoons chocolate sirup to 1 cup milk, chilled; beat with rotary beater and pour into tall glass. Add small scoop of chocolate or coffee ice cream, stir slightly with spoon and serve at once. Serves 1.

Chocolate Malted Milk

Use 2 tablespoons each malted milk powder and chocolate sirup to 1 cup milk; beat with rotary beater or shake until frothy; pour over cracked ice in tall glass and serve at once. Serves 1.

Various Drinks
for Various
Tastes

CIDER

Various Drinks

Egg Nog

    8 egg yolks
    6 tablespoons sugar
    2 quarts milk
    Rum flavoring, to taste
    8 egg whites
    Nutmeg

Beat egg yolks; add sugar. Add milk and
Rum extract. Beat egg whites stiff; fold
in. Pour into tall glasses; sprinkle with
nutmeg. Serves 8.

Baltimore Egg Nog

    12 eggs
    1 pound sugar
    Rum extract, to taste
    3 pints milk
    1 pint cream

Beat yolks to a foam, add the Rum extract slowly, then the sugar, stirring
constantly. Then add the milk and
cream and, finally, fold in the stiffly
beaten wihtes.

Kentucky Egg Nog

12 eggs   1 pint milk
2 pounds sugar   3 pints cream
Rum or Brandy flavoring, to taste

Beat yolks, beat in the sugar, then slowly stir in the flavoring. Stir in the milk and cream. Fold in the stiffly beaten whites.

Western Egg Nog

12 eggs
½ pound sugar
Brandy flavoring, to taste
3 pints heavy cream

Beat the yolks to a froth and beat in the sugar. Slowly stir in the Brandy flavoring. Whip the cream and stir it into the mixture. Beat the whites until light, but not stiff, and stir them into the mixture.

Coffee Egg Nog

2 eggs
¼ cup granulated sugar
3 tablespoons instant-coffee powder
3 cups milk
Grated orange rind or chocolate

Separate eggs; place whites in small

bowl, yolks in medium bowl. With hand beater or electric mixer, beat whites till they form peaks when beater is raised. Gradually add sugar, then 1 tablespoon instant coffee. Beat till stiff. Set aside. Beat yolks with remaining 2 tablespoons instant coffee; add about 1/3 cup milk; beat till smooth. Add rest of milk. Fold in egg-white mixture till frothy. Serve in tall glasses, with sprinkling of rind. Makes 6 servings.

Almond Egg Nog

10 eggs
10 tablespoons sugar
¾ teaspoon salt
2 ½ quarts hot milk
2 ½ teaspoons vanilla extract
2 ½ teaspoons almond extract

Beat eggs. Gradually beat in sugar and salt. Slowly add hot milk. Flavor with vanilla and almond extract. Beat until frothy. Serve hot in tall glasses dusted with freshly ground nutmeg. Serves 10.

Chocolate Egg Nog

Flavor Egg Nog with chocolate sirup, using 2 tablespoons for each glass.

Individual Egg Nog

   1 egg
   1 teaspoon sugar
   1 teaspoon Rum extract
   8 ounces milk

Shake vigorously with cracked ice, strain into a tall glass, and serve with a dash of nutmeg over the top.

Single measure . . . .
Double pleasure

Orgeat

4 quarts milk
2 sticks cinnamon
4 tablespoons rose water
½ cup sugar
½ cup (6 ounces) almonds

Add cinnamon to milk and bring gradually to boiling point. Remove cinnamon and allow milk to cool. Blanch almonds, pound to a paste in a mortar. Add rose water to chopped almonds. Add to milk, mixing well. Sweeten to taste and heat for a minute or two only. Strain through fine sieve or cheesecloth. Serves 12.

Ginger Ale Cream

⅓ cup lemon juice
1 banana, mashed
½ cup sugar
½ cup medium cream
½ pint orange ice
1 pint ginger ale, chilled
1 orange, sliced

Combine lemon juice, banana and sugar and chill; stir in cream, add orange ice and ginger ale. Mix well and decorate with orange slices. Yields 4 cups.

Mock Tom and Jerry

12 eggs
½ pound sugar
Rum flavoring, to taste
1 tablespoon each ground allspice,
  cinnamon and cloves

Beat yolks and whites separately. Beat in the sugar and spices with yolks, then pour in the Rum flavoring gradually, stirring constantly. Finally, fold in the whites. Store this in a large bowl.

Put a ladleful of the mixture in a large mug, fill mug with boiling water or hot milk, and stir vigorously until the whole drink foams. Dust with ground nutmeg if desired.

Grape Juice Froth

3 tablespoons orange juice
½ cup grape juice
2 teaspoons sugar
Dash of salt
1 egg white, stiffly beaten

Pour chilled fruit juices in tall glass; add sugar and salt to stiffly beaten egg white, add to fruit juice and stir just enough to mix well. Serves 1.

Rail Splitter

One ounce sugar sirup, juice of 1 medium-sized lemon. Fill up glass with ginger ale over cracked ice.

Saratoga Cooler

Ginger ale and sarsaparilla, half and half.
Also called a Saratoga: the Rail Splitter
plus a few dashes of Angostura.

Horse's Neck

Peel a medium or large lemon in one
continuous spiral. Hang the peel in a
tall glass with just enough over the edge
to keep the peel in place. Place 3 or 4
large cubes of ice in the glass and fill
with ginger ale. A teetotaller's highball!

Prohibition Fizz

Grape juice, Grenadine. Orgeat, or any
fruit sirup, frappéd with lime or lemon
juice and fizzed up with charged water.
Makes a mighty refreshing drink.

Rhubarb Flip

Stir 1 cup sweetened rhubarb juice, 1
tablespoon sugar and dash of nutmeg
into 3 well-beaten egg yolks and pour
over cracked ice in 6 tall glasses. Fill
with ginger ale and serve at once.

Frosted Root Beer

This is easiest made with a blender, but it also can be done with a rotary beater. For each person allow 4 ounces of root beer and a half cup vanilla ice cream. Beat together until entirely combined. Other sparkling drinks may of course be used.

Chilled Spiced Cider

Bring to a boil 1 quart of cider with a stick of cinnamon, 6 whole cloves, 4 allspice berries, and 2 tablespoons of honey. Lower heat and simmer for 15 minutes. Strain and chill. In each highball glass put 2 or 3 cubes of ice. Fill glass half with cider mixture and half with club soda.

Grape Juice

Instead of the usual tomato juice cocktail, serve as first course with a light luncheon a frosty grape-juice drink. It is made most simply from a frozen concentrate; a bit of fresh lime juice may be added for a sharper flavor.

Grapefruit-Mint Drink

Stir ½ cup sugar and ½ cup water in a saucepan over direct heat until sugar is dissolved. Remove from stove and add a cupful of mint leaves. Crush the leaves in the sirup and let stand 1 hour. Strain. Add ½ cup grapefruit juice, 2 tablespoons lime juice and ½ cup water. Chill. Just before serving, add 2 cups of ginger ale.

Spiced Fruit Nectar

2 ½ cups orange juice
2 teaspoons grated lemon rind
3 tablespoons lemon juice
1 ½ cups pineapple juice
2 cups water
6 whole cloves
½ teaspoon nutmeg
¼ teaspoon allspice
½ teaspoon cinnamon
½ cup sugar
1 tablespoon honey
1 ½ quarts ginger ale

Combine orange juice, lemon rind and juice, pineapple juice, water, spices, sugar and honey; cover and let stand in warm place 3 hours. Strain over cracked

ice; add ginger ale and serve at once.
Yields 24 small glasses.

Spicy Iced Chocolate

    6 tablespoons cocoa
    1 cup boiling water
    8 sprigs mint, washed
    2 cans evaporated milk
    1 stick cinnamon
    ¼ cup sugar

Stir cocoa to a paste with a little of the
boiling water, add remaining water and
4 sprigs of mint and cook until thick,
stirring constantly. Add remaining ingredients and bring to boiling point,
stirring constantly. Remove mint, pour
over cracked ice and add a sprig of fresh
mint to each glass. Approximate yield:
4 portions.

Cider Mint Cocktail

    2 cups sweet cider
    ½ cup pineapple juice
    ½ cup orange juice

Combine all ingredients, strain and chill.
Serve in cocktail glasses and garnish each
with a sprig of mint. May be used as a
before-dinner appetizer. Serves 6.

Fruit Fizz

Combine equal amounts of fruit juice
and ginger ale, or use charged water and
sirup. Add the carbonated beverage just
before serving, and pour over ice cubes
or cracked ice.